The S.C.U.B.A. Approach: Dive Deep Into Your Child's Behavior

By Kristene Geering, M.A.

Edited by Lisa D. Thompson

Copyright © 2024 by Kristene Geering

Thank you for complying with copyright laws and not duplicating or reproducing any portion of this book in any form without written permission from the publisher or author, except as permitted by U.S. copyright law. All rights reserved.

This publication is designed to give readers a general framework in which to understand behavior, but should not be used as a diagnostic tool or substitute for professional support. Neither the publisher nor the author should be construed as offering individualized advice or services. If you need further support, please seek out a licensed, certified or credentialed professional as appropriate.

Published by Let Us Learn Together

To my children, who have taught me far more than I could ever teach them.

Table of Contents

Introduction 1
See 5
Child 13
Under 19
Behavior 23
Adapt 26
Not Just For Kids 37
Putting It Into Practice 40
Conclusion 59
Your Turn! 61
My Cup-Fillers 66
Sensory Input Ideas 68
Resources 77

Introduction

You're in the cereal aisle, trying to juggle a gallon of milk, a carton of eggs and your 3-year-old, who's insisted on walking "like a big boy" rather than ride like a "baby" in the cart. You turn your back for a second to gingerly place eggs in the cart, and BAM—a crash from behind almost makes you drop the whole dozen. Your big boy has just knocked several cereal boxes to the floor, and now every pair of eyes in the store is on you, judging you and finding your parenting wanting.

****

Your family is at your in-laws for a holiday meal. Your mother-in-law was in the kitchen most of the day, cooking up a storm, and you know the effort she went to—but your 7-year-old doesn't. She's wiggling in the chair, softly singing a song about how gross the mashed potatoes are. Grandma looks insulted and says, "Stop complaining and eat your food." Your child looks up, astonished, then yells, "You're gross!" Everyone stops and stares. You desperately wish for an invisibility cloak, mortified.

****

Your 12-year-old comes home from school and dumps their backpack smack dab in the middle of the floor. You ask her (nicely) to pick it up and put it on the hook where it belongs. She bursts into tears and starts screaming, "You're always yelling at me! You don't understand anything! I hate you!" Then she runs to her room and slams the door. You stand in the middle of the living room, hurt and confused.

****

Maybe you've never experienced one of these exact scenarios, but you've probably had at least a few occasions when your child's behavior made you cringe while you felt the judgment of the world crash down upon you. Our children's behaviors can be a mystery at the best of times and a total catastrophe at the worst. Kids are weird, right? And if you're tired and frazzled and just trying to get through the regular stuff of the day, a blowout or meltdown can become the stuff of nightmares.

Let me assure you that your kid is not trying to make your life a living hell. There *are* reasons behind their behaviors. A child's behavior is actually a form of communication—a kind of language to let the adults in the room see what's going on with that kid.

Most adults have a really hard time understanding that language. Why? Because the behavior itself is just the tip of the iceberg. It's all we see, so it's what we respond to. But the truth is there is *a lot* going on beneath the surface. Once you have an idea of what's actually happening inside them, you can understand what their behavior is trying to say—which means you're more able to support your kid and help them shift their behavior to something more socially acceptable.

Understanding your kid's behavior can be tricky. You might see the same behavior, from the same kid, in the same place, at a different time—and find that what worked to shift things last time doesn't work the next. Remember that icebergs drift! There are so many variables and factors in each situation, it can seem impossible for a parent to know what the right thing to do is in the moment.

First things first: There is rarely one "right" thing to do at any moment. There is no perfect way to parent, no matter what you read on social media. We are human beings, and we are all perfectly imperfect, flawed in ways unique to each of us. This chaotic mosaic is in a constant flux, making sure that no matter what else we may experience as parents, boredom will rarely be in the mix.

So, what can you do? How do you even begin to approach unwanted behaviors from your kid when the landscape is constantly changing? This is where the S.C.U.B.A. approach comes in.

The S.C.U.B.A. approach is a quick and easy way to remember what to do in the moment, why you should do it, and how it can be done. While no one method will get you the perfect response every time (keep in mind there is no such thing as perfect in parenting), this flexible framework not only gives you permission to experiment to see what works, it also creates a relationship between you and your child that promotes safety, closeness, and a lifetime of trust.

After practicing this approach, you'll be more in tune with your child, confident in your parenting, and compassionate with your child, yourself, and others.

The S.C.U.B.A. approach:

See the
Child
Under the
Behavior, then
Adapt

We'll drill down into each part of this approach throughout the rest of the book. Get your goggles, and let's dive.

See

Your kiddo is screaming on the floor of the cereal aisle. Again. In a panic you try to figure out what to do when it hits you: Take a deep breath, and look beneath the surface.

It's time for the S.C.U.B.A. approach. Let's talk about the first part: See.

Yes, you want to see your sweet child (remember them?) under that awful behavior, but seeing in this instance also means to take a closer look and observe. Your observations in the moment will be your vital clues as to what you can try next. Specifically, there are three things to take in:

- *Physiological cues*
- *Environmental cues*
- *Time-related cues*

Physiological cues

These are what your child's body is trying to say. It's easy to get overwhelmed in these tough moments as we worry about our kid, or what everyone around us is thinking, or how we'll get to our appointment on time. But when our kid is acting out in some way, what's really happening is a form of communication. As parents, our job is to decipher that language.

Often when kids act out it's because they're in their fight-or-flight mode; they're detecting a threat somewhere. Is it objectively a threat that they can't have the Sugar-Os? No. No, it is not.

But remember their brain is pretty under-baked, especially in early childhood. Just because we don't understand why they're feeling unsafe, it doesn't negate their feelings.

I compare this to how I feel when I see a spider. My husband cannot comprehend why I'm screaming bloody murder as I bolt out of a room when I spot an arachnid. But him telling me, "You're not being rational," doesn't take away the fact that I have a phobia that floods me with irrational fear. My stress response is triggered because of how *I feel,* not because of what brand of spider it is. I communicate that fear with my physiological cues—screaming and running.

That stress response manifests in a lot of ways, not just fight or flight. There's also freeze or faint, which can be literally fainting or generally shutting down. Basically, the body gathers its resources to get ready for a fight, flight, freeze or faint response in order to survive. There are some great resources out there explaining more about what's going on during this process (I highly recommend *Brain-Body Parenting* and *The Whole-Brain Child*), but in a tough moment with your kid, you just need to know what cues to look for that signal a stress response—when they need connection and comfort, *not* correction. Here are some things to look for:

- Increased heart rate
- Rapid or shallow breathing
- Flushed or pale skin
- Dilated pupils
- Sweating
- Fisted hands
- Clenched jaw
- Trembling or shaking
- Upset stomach
- Tapping fingers
- Running or trying to get away
- Avoiding eye contact
- Shrinking back or making themselves smaller
- Freezing in place
- Headache
- Stomach ache
- Crying
- Screaming
- Rapid speech
- Stuttering
- Inability to speak clearly
- Withdrawing or shutting down

An exhaustive list would be, well, exhausting to read, let alone remember. In essence, what you're looking for are cues that your kiddo is feeling unsafe. Part of this process is getting to know your child more deeply. Over time, you'll be able to see a specific behavior and instantly know that they're in a full-blown stress response. As you become more adept at observing your child, you'll even start picking up clues when they're about to lose it so you can intervene early. Then, as your child grows, you'll be able to alert them to their cues, so they can take action themselves and avoid the freak-out all together. Powerful stuff, this observation!

Environmental Cues

The next thing to tune in to is your surroundings. Very often, adults will miss cues that something is stressful to a kid simply because we're adults and don't have a child's perspective anymore. One of the easiest ways to organize your thoughts on this is to think about your child's senses and how the environment might impact them. If you consider all eight senses (I'll detail them all below), it can help you shift your perspective.

Sight

Look around you and take in what you see. Is it busy or overwhelming? Bland and boring? Make sure you get down on your child's level, too. The view from two feet above the floor is different from your view above. If you get down on the floor in that cereal aisle, for instance, you'll have a very different perspective on just how many shapes and colors are screaming out at you. No wonder your kiddo is melting!

Sound

Close your eyes and listen for a moment. Take note of the sounds in the background that your grown-up brain may have filtered out. It might be that your child's not yet able to distinguish what sounds are important, and so they are inundated by all the sounds. Maybe there's a higher pitched or a louder sound, and you realize that your child had trouble the last time that sound was there. Air dryers in public bathrooms are a great example of this. As adults we just filter out that loud whooshing sound, but kids are often startled and frightened by the sudden and intense noise.

Smell

With your eyes still closed, shift your attention to your nose. Are there any particularly strong smells around you? Kids' senses can be more sensitive than adults', and a scent that may seem faint or even pleasant to you might overwhelm your child.

Touch

Take a moment to do a quick inventory of everything that's touching your child. That means clothes (tags on shirts, pants and undies are notoriously challenging for a lot of kids). It means socks (another famous irritant). It means shoes (those tiny feet grow and those little shoes don't). Think about the surface they're sitting/lying on: Is it carpeted or hard and smooth? Is it textured? Rough? Also think of temperature: Is it hot or cold? Remember that even if it doesn't bother you, that doesn't mean your child is overreacting. It means that their brain and body are different than yours, and they need help dealing in the moment.

Taste

This is tied in pretty strongly to smell, but if the meltdown is happening at a meal, sometimes this is a vital clue. Strong flavors of sour, salty, spicy, and even sweet can be too much for tiny tongues. Take a moment to consider what your child might be tasting in a stressful moment and if that could be impacting their behavior.

Balance (Vestibular Sense)

This might be a new one for you, but our sense of balance is often considered one of our general senses. This sense lets you know how your head is oriented in space—like, if you're upside down or rightside up. You probably know how disorienting it can be when you feel dizzy. Sometimes it can be fun, and sometimes it's scary or unnerving. Kids who have been playing at the park might feel a little off-balance, and so might kids suffering from an ear infection. Both scenarios can lead to unwanted behaviors.

Body Position (Proprioception)

This might be another new one for you. Basically, it means your sense of body position—whether you're sitting or standing, or if your legs are crossed or not, for example. Our brain gets that information from receptors that sense pressure throughout our body. It can be really dysregulating when you don't know where your body is, but it can be pretty hard to describe when you feel it. If you are in an area that's crowded and your little one is being bumped around or squished, that can feel very disorienting and threatening to them.

Internal Sensations (Interoception)

This sense is how your brain interprets information from its internal environment—whether your bladder is full or your stomach is empty, for example. Very often, children may not know how to interpret those signals, leading to their brain giving danger vibes. Think of the child who forgets to eat, goes way too long without food, and then explodes into a full-blown hangry tantrum. (Newsflash: We don't outgrow hangry.)

Time-Related Cues

Last but not least, you always want to notice what time of day it is during a stress response. Meltdowns are much more likely to happen toward the end of the day—the "witching hour," as it's often called. This is largely because kids are really tired by this time of day, and it's harder for them to keep it together. Likewise, note the timing around meals or eating. If you realize that lunch is later than usual and your kid is freaking out because you gave them the blue bowl and not the red, it might be a hangry response that you're dealing with, not a color battle. Other time-related cues might include bathroom breaks, after-school or other activities (maybe they just had a challenging class or performance), and early mornings, when waking up can be a challenge.

Child

There are actually three things I want you to think about when we talk about the "child" part of the S.C.U.B.A. approach: your love, your child, and the relationship you share. All three of these things can influence how you see your child in any given moment, especially during tough ones.

First, focus on the love you feel for your child.
This might seem like a "duh" statement, but stay with me. You love your child. You would walk through fire for them. You sacrifice so much, all the time, for their well-being and happiness. Of course you love them!

Yet, in that moment—that horrible moment when they've lost their mind and you're about to lose yours—that love gets buried. It gets buried underneath the anger and the hurt and the stress of just getting through that moment. Sometimes it feels like your child is being intentionally stubborn, that they're trying to hurt you. And we forget and lash out from a place of anger and pain and stress instead of a place of love.

So, get yourself into the habit of taking a moment to appreciate just how much you love your kid when you see them. Take a beat to appreciate their little nose, or the softness of their hair, or the way their hand feels in yours. For older kids, lean in to that feeling of joy when they accomplish something new, or have a shared moment of laughter. The more practiced you are at consciously loving your child, the easier it will be to find that emotion even during times of stress.

Next, think about your child and their development. First and foremost, remember that the front part of your kid's brain, the part that's in control of regulating or controlling emotions, is not finished yet. I don't even have to know how old your child is. The fact that they aren't an adult means it's not finished yet.

The younger they are, the more under-developed their prefrontal cortex is. This means that for a 3- or 4-year-old, tantrums aren't just normal—they're expected! Just like your toddler fell down over and over while they learned how to walk, very young children will melt down over and over while they learn how to regulate their emotions. This is why our job as parents is to *co-regulate* with our children. Or as I like to say, our job is to let our kids borrow our brains for a little while.

The calmer we are in the moment, the more quickly our kids will be able to calm down. The more grounded we are in the midst of the storm, the faster they'll be able to pull it back together. We'll talk more about this when we get into the Adapt section, but it's important to put a pin in it now.

Speaking of younger children, that inability to regulate their emotions means they get frustrated much more quickly. And since they're still learning so many new things, we get front row seats to that frustration on a daily basis. Motor skills like walking are pretty complicated to learn. Of course they're going to fall down a lot, and of course they'll be frustrated when they can't get to that toy you're holding just out of reach. Those tiny bodies get tired pretty quickly, too, so when you add frustration in, well, it isn't surprising those unwanted behaviors erupt so quickly (and loudly).

Another example of this is language and communication, one of the most common triggers for outbursts in young children. While our brains have evolved to understand language almost from birth, it still takes a few years for all those systems to come online. If you've ever tried to order something in a language you're just learning, you know how frustrating it is when no one understands you. Add in the fact that the front part of the brain can't really handle emotions yet, and you've got the recipe for a humdinger of a tantrum.

Developmental skills across the spectrum are triggers for challenging behaviors. Self-help skills are huge when kids are young—think of the kindergartner who wants to tie their shoes, "By myself!" even though you were supposed to be at the doctor's office five minutes ago. And when those skills are first coming online, they're not very reliable. Your kid can tie their shoes fine one day, but the next it's like they've forgotten everything. While this is definitely cause for outbursts on your part as well as theirs, it's worth remembering that these emerging skills take a while to set. It's the same as when they kept falling down as toddlers—it takes time, practice, and lots of failure before we make that next big developmental leap from one stage to the next.

Lastly, consider the uniqueness of *this kid* and your relationship with them.
As a parent of twins, I can tell you firsthand that even if two kids are the same age—even if they've been in the same environment since conception—no two children are exactly the same. So when a meltdown or tantrum erupts, take a beat and consider this particular kiddo and their behavior. Is this something that happens often for them? Is it expected or a surprise?

Remember how important it was to see the environmental cues and think about how your child's senses took in information? When you combine that knowledge with understanding that every brain and body is unique, you start to get a deeper insight into your specific child and why they might have this behavior when other kids don't. This starts to dip into something called sensory processing, or sensory integration. That's how your brain makes sense of all those different streams of input. Again, young brains have a lot of baking yet to do, and they're not as good at integrating all of that information to make sense of the world.

Some kids are really sensitive to loud sounds, and some don't seem to notice them at all. Some kids are slow to understand internal senses like hunger or a full bladder, which may lead that child to being hangry more often, or slower to potty train. By tuning in to the environment and seeing how your child reacts, you're starting to build this superpower of tuning in to *your* kid. And that is going to guide you when it comes time to adapt.

Take some time to really study your child. What do they like or dislike? Are they particularly sensitive to anything? Or are they missing some cues? Do they have any fears? If so, what helps to calm those fears? How might this child respond differently than a friend or sibling in a similar situation?

As you learn more about your child and how they react to different situations, you'll find the added benefit of helping your child feel loved and supported, of feeling seen and understood. This helps to build the relationship between the two of you and to strengthen your bond. In certain circles, that bond is also referred to as their "attachment," and having a secure attachment is something that research shows leads to better outcomes for kids for the rest of their lives.

A secure attachment means your child sees you as their safe haven and secure base. More than just feeling loved and supported, it means they feel worthy of that love and support, so as they go out into the world, they have more confidence and resilience. It helps them feel safer, which lets them explore and learn more.

And secure attachment leads to happier relationships. It's even been linked to better academic performance and higher incomes. In fact, of all the things you can do to help your child grow into a confident, happy adult, creating a secure attachment gives you more metaphorical bang for your buck than anything else.

Under

The behaviors that we see are just the tip of the iceberg. Our job as parents is to take a deeper dive and learn about what's going on under the surface. This is where you use all of the information you gathered while you were observing the moment.

For example, remember that cereal aisle we talked about? Your 3-year-old, who insisted on helping push the grocery cart, is now on the floor pitching a fit. Someone nearby mumbles something like, "Spoiled brat throwing a fit because they want something." You take a breath and **SEE** the situation, observing the following:

- Your child's face is red and they're taking heaving breaths in between screams.
- The store is more crowded than usual because of a sale.
- It's almost naptime.

You take another deep breath, think about your **CHILD**, and remember:

- You love your kid.
- Their brain has not yet developed enough to control big emotions.

- Your child was woken up earlier than usual that morning.
- While they really do love the cereal that they're screaming about, they don't usually pitch a fit like this.

So, it seems that all things are pointing to something else going on **UNDER** the surface.

See where we're going with this? We're now at the S.C.U. part of S.C.U.B.A.

You realized that *underneath* this hissy fit, your kid is not a spoiled brat. They're obviously overwhelmed by feelings they can't control. They're also probably more tired than usual. In other words, when you look beneath the surface (or the floor of the cereal aisle, in this instance), you understand what's causing this behavior, and you're able to find empathy.

The empathy piece is pretty important, as that goes toward building that relationship (secure attachment). Think of it this way: Imagine you were late to work because you got stopped for a ticket. You spilled coffee on yourself moments before an important meeting. Your friend made reservations for lunch, but on the way you realize you have to stop for gas. As you're running into the restaurant, 20 minutes late, an unexpected storm rolls in and you get soaked in the parking lot. When you finally get to your table, your friend says, "I have been planning this for weeks. How can you be this late? And look at you! You're a mess! So disrespectful!"

How would you feel about that friend? Do you feel closer to them? Probably not. Chances are that relationship would be strained for a while. But what if your friend responded like this?

"I'm so glad you could make it! Oh, wow. It looks like you've had a rough day. Wanna talk about it?" They get up to give you a hug even though you're soaking wet, smile as you both sit down, and then listen as you unload.

How do you feel about your friend now? What does that response do to your relationship?

In the day-to-day cascade of schedules and responsibilities, it can be easy to forget that our kids are people, too. They're just smaller people, and because they're still growing, they need a lot of help. When we take that breath and look underneath the surface of a challenging behavior, we have the opportunity to connect with our kid and to see who they truly are in the moment. More than that, when we help them feel supported underneath their challenges and successes alike, we get glimpses of who they are becoming and how we influence that one way or another.

Tip: Also look underneath the surface of your own behavior.

I can't count how many times I've seen parents not even consider what they bring to a situation. Often when we find our kid's behavior bothersome, it has as much (if not more) to do with ourselves than it does with them.

Back to the tantrum in the cereal aisle. Consider these questions: *Why does their meltdown bother you so much? Are you feeling judged by those around you? Do you have bad memories of how your own parents handled your tantrums? Are you just as sensitive to loud sounds as your child?*

A big part of diving deep for that empathy is looking inward. If you find yourself triggered in the moment for a specific reason, looking inward not only helps you manage your own emotions, it gives you insight into what might be going on with your child. "Oh," you might think, "I can't stand that screaming! It really hurts my ears, and I want to make it stop or get away from it! Huh. Now that I think about it, I wonder if my kid feels the same."

Behavior

You're building your observation skills. You're starting to understand your child on a deeper level, both developmentally and as an individual. You're open to taking that deep dive so you can see what's going on underneath the behavior that's bothering you.

So, let's stop there and define behavior—what does that really mean? What encompasses behavior? Many times in my practice, I've heard parents say things like, "She's acting out," or, "I can't stand the backtalk," or, "He just won't listen!" To which I always respond, "Tell me more."

I always want to know more because, while these are common ways to describe a challenging situation, they don't give me much information about what the behavior is exactly. What does acting out mean to you? Or backtalk? When you say he won't listen, do you mean he won't take off his headphones or that he won't obey you?

This is where those observational skills come in handy once more. Imagine you have to describe your child's behavior to someone who has never seen it before, or hasn't even met your kid. What is your kid actually doing? Are they hitting the floor? Kicking the door? Are they rolling their eyes and crossing their arms? Are they asking questions like, "Why should I?" The more objectively you can describe the behavior, the more you can a) start to separate those physiological responses from willful behaviors, b) isolate what willful behaviors you want them to change, and c) understand your own responses and reactions.

For example, if someone says, "He won't listen to me!" and I ask for more information, I might learn a few things:

- He is actually listening, he's just refusing to do what was asked.
- When he refuses, he crosses his arms, avoids eye contact, and clenches his jaw.
- He says, "Why do I have to do it? I hate doing that!"
- His parent feels disrespected and unappreciated and ends up yelling and punishing every time.

I also want to know what happened right before the behavior. What was the setup? If the child in the cereal aisle was pushing the shopping cart, could that have made her more tired? Was the boy refusing to do what he was asked in the middle of a favorite show or game?

The other important thing to consider is what happens immediately after. Going back to the child in the cereal aisle: Did her parent comfort her? Pick her up and remove her from the store? Give in and put the cereal into the cart?

By knowing what happened before, during, and after challenging behaviors, you set yourself and your child up for an easier time when you're in that situation again.

Adapt

I like using the acronym S.C.U.B.A. because it's an easy way to help you remember the steps of handling challenging behaviors with your child. It helps you remember to See your Child Under the Behavior, which we just talked about— then Adapt.

Specifically, it has you ask yourself these questions:

1. **What do I *see*? What cues can I observe?**
2. **What's happening with my *child*? Both developmentally and individually?**
3. **What do I think is *under* their behavior? What needs aren't being met?**
4. **What, exactly, is the *behavior*? What's happening before, during, and after?**

And now we're going to ask the question that allows us to put what we've learned into action:

5. **What can I *adapt* or change? How can I help?**

What to Do

Now that you've gathered information from the first four questions, it's time to dive into the last part: adapting. What, exactly, are you supposed to do with what you've learned? That will vary, depending on your observations, how well you understand your child, and the specifics of the behavior and situation. In general, though, there are some levers you can pull to switch things up.

Change the Environment

If you've observed that your child doesn't do well in loud places, you might choose to avoid events like concerts or crowded markets. If there's a tantrum every time you go down the cereal aisle, you might choose to skip that aisle for a while—or maybe be sure your child is in the cart instead of pushing it. Especially for younger children, a simple change to the environment can go a long way in preventing unwanted behaviors.

Manage Sensory Input

If loud places are an important part of your family life and can't be avoided, you can try headphones to reduce the noise. If your child is sensitive to light, sunglasses or a hat can be helpful. Maybe you've observed that your child has a hard time recognizing internal cues like hunger, and getting hangry is a regular occurrence. Using a timer to make sure they get a snack when they need it can keep tantrums at bay.

You can also use these tools to help manage behavior on a more general level. Let's say you've been studying your child and you notice they really like crashing into things and bear hugs (proprioception). You might make sure they have that input on a regular basis through things like wheelbarrow walks or bouncing on a mini trampoline. If you have a kiddo who seems calmer after vestibular activities like swinging, maybe you put a small swing in the corner or make sure you get to the park every morning for time on the merry-go-round. You can use scents you know your child finds soothing, like lavender or chamomile, to help wind down at bedtime.

Developing a deeper understanding of how your child uses their senses to make sense of the world is one of the most helpful, least-known tools parents have. I can't tell you how many times I've seen small adaptations to daily activities make huge changes in the lives of families. I've added some resources at the end of this book where you can take notes based on your observations.

Shift Your Tone

It's easy to feel frustrated, overwhelmed, and/or triggered by our kids. It's part of being human! But when we let those feelings seep into how we talk to our kids, we end up hindering our connection to them rather than helping it.

Taking a pause to breathe, ground yourself, and regulate your own emotions—whatever it is you need to do so that you can take a step back from the moment—is another great way to help build that ever-important secure attachment in your child. I also know how hard it can be to do that, especially when you're already triggered. This is why taking the time to fill your own cup is critical.

Taking care of yourself is taking care of your child. Let me repeat that: Taking care of yourself is taking care of your child.

I've added a resource in the back to help you identify what that means to you. And remember, it doesn't need to be huge! While a week (or four) on a solo vacation at the spa is absolutely one way to recharge, you can get the same benefits from frequent, smaller acts that happen regularly throughout the day.

Also, keep in mind that the expectation here isn't that you do this perfectly. In fact, there's no such thing as "perfect parenting," no matter what you heard on social media. There is, however, research on a concept called "good enough parenting." What does this mean? That you're going to make mistakes. How do I know? Because you're human. The thing is, those mistakes are also opportunities to do something called "repair."

When we slip up and yell or say something we regret in the moment, we get the chance to show our kids how to make it right. We can calm down, go back, apologize, and let them know how we'll try to do things differently next time.

This can be a profound shift in tone for some folks, especially for those who never had their own parents model how to do this. But think, for a moment, just how profound these moments can be for our kids. When we show our kids how to own their mistakes, make amends, and repair important relationships, we're giving them a template for their future relationships with friends, partners, spouses, and eventually maybe kids of their own.

Adjust Expectations

I don't know how many times I've heard both parents and teachers tell a child who is in a full-blown tantrum to "use your words!" This is where understanding your child's development is critical. It also helps to understand how human brains work, in general.

First, let's talk brains. Remember how you can observe if a child's stress response has been activated based on physiological cues, like a flushed face, shrinking back, avoiding eye contact, etc? That stress response, in children and adults alike, essentially cuts off communication between that higher, logical, thinking part of the brain and the lower, survival-oriented part. Dr. Dan Siegel refers to this as the "upstairs" and "downstairs" brain. Things like words and reason are in that upstairs part—and if the downstairs part is driving, there's just no accessing them.

A few years ago, I had a very severe asthma attack that put me in an ambulance and landed me in the hospital for a few days (I had a full recovery). While I was lying on my bed, literally gasping for air, the paramedics kept asking me questions and telling me to breathe. My brain was pretty well developed at that time. I was an adult. But in that moment, there was no way on earth I could even breathe, let alone answer their questions.

I can laugh about it now, but it serves as a reminder to me of how important it is to recognize when my kids are having a stress response. Physiological cues give me important information, and I know that I cannot expect them to "use their words" in that moment. Instead, I need to help them feel safer, so they can move out of that stress response. Offering comfort during those moments not only helps to build that secure attachment (I am their safe haven). It also literally helps their brains reconfigure, so they can use all the tools we've spent so long building together.

Now let's talk development. If you expect your very young child to control their emotions, that's literally an unrealistic expectation—the region of their brain that controls emotions isn't developed yet, so they physically cannot do as you'd wish. Game-changer, right? Likewise, when you understand how things like organization or time management are also developmental skills, it can help reduce your frustration when your kid forgets about homework assignments or has trouble keeping their room tidy. When we adjust our expectations to align with our child's development—and then help them learn and practice their budding skills instead of punishing them for things that are literally beyond their control—everyone wins.

Reinforce Boundaries

Finally, understanding how boundaries affect behavior can be helpful for parents, as well. In general, I see two reasons that children push against boundaries:

- They want to know you'll hold that boundary because it helps them feel safe.

- The boundary no longer serves them developmentally, and it needs to be adjusted.

First, boundaries are important because they help kids feel safe. I like to think of them like a fence. Imagine a yard with a fence all the way around it. You know that everything inside that fence is safe for your kid—there are no poisonous plants, the play equipment is safe, no sharp objects, etc. Outside that fence, though, you have no idea if it's safe or not. So, of course, you keep that fence up! And because that fence is there, your child feels safe to explore and learn within those boundaries. They might push against the fence or even try to climb over it, but you will step in every single time to direct them back to the area you know is safe.

Fun fact: Some kids will do that A LOT. Like, over and over and over. It's okay—you just keep holding that boundary. Over time, they'll learn to trust that you will be there to help them stay safe. They'll learn that you are their secure base and safe haven. That secure attachment will build and grow.

There comes a time, however, when boundaries need to move. When I was a senior in high school, I was going to my senior prom, and my mother told me my curfew was 10:00 p.m. I told her the dance didn't even start till 9:00 p.m. She held the boundary, and told me, "Your curfew is 10:00 p.m." But I pushed back, stating it didn't feel reasonable, given that I was going to move out in a few weeks and be on my own at college. After a conversation with her, she adjusted the boundary and moved the curfew.

The bottom line here is that, as parents, we need to see our kids for who they are in the moment, as well as where they are in their development. Based on those observations, we need to ask ourselves if our expectations are reasonable. If not, we can adapt and adjust.

No One Right Way

Keep in mind that parenting is part science, part art, and part shifting sand— it's continually changing as your child grows. This means there is never one right answer to any situation. It might even be that the same behavior needs different responses at different times. That's where the S.C.U.B.A. approach comes in.

Let's take this scenario: Your first grader is having regular meltdowns after school. You go through the five questions:

1. What do I *see*? What cues can I observe?
    You observe he's crying and unable to use his words.

2. What's happening with my *child*? Both developmentally and individually?

You know that he, unlike his sister, has a hard time recognizing when he's hungry and that he easily gets hangry. You also know that he's only 6 years old and isn't able to control his emotions easily yet.

3. What do I think is *under* this behavior? What needs aren't being met?
You suspect that what's really going on is that he's hungry after school.

4. What, exactly, is the *behavior*? What's happening before, during, and after?
He's suddenly getting upset over something that doesn't usually bother him, crumpling to the floor, screaming, crying, and lashing out at anyone who gets near him. You know that he's been at school all day, plus sat in the car for the long ride home right before. Afterward, you've been feeling frustrated and trying to pretend it didn't happen.

5. What can I *adapt* or change? How can I help?
You decide you'll adapt by having a snack ready for him to eat in the car when you get him from school.

You are pleasantly surprised when two weeks go by without a single meltdown—yay snacks!

But in the third week, it starts again. He's having meltdowns every day after school, even with the snack. So, you go back to the five questions, this time asking for more input from the teacher.

You learn that the kids have had to have indoor recess this week due to weather. You know that your son is a kid who needs a lot of movement and sensory input, so you give him extra time to jump on the trampoline and or play on the swing you have at home as soon as you get home from school. The meltdowns stop again.

Our kids continue to grow and change, as does their environment and schedule. By consistently addressing any challenging behaviors with the S.C.U.B.A. approach, you're giving yourself and your child what you need to create a deeper bond. You're also figuring out the root causes of troubling behaviors in a way that's respectful of you both.

The S.C.U.B.A. approach sets you and your child up for more snuggles and less screaming, for more parenting confidence and fewer regrets, with grace and space for growth and learning for everyone. And this lays the foundation for a secure relationship that you'll both enjoy as your kid transforms from a child into a young adult and beyond.

Not Just for Kids

When you go through the steps I just outlined, you're doing more than just addressing behavior that drives you crazy; you're letting your child know you're there. You're helping them feel seen and safe. You're building their confidence and their resilience. All of these things happen as part of the special relationship and secure attachment that you're intentionally building.

But these steps can work with anyone you have a relationship with—including yourself.

One "muscle" the S.C.U.B.A. approach builds is that of compassion. By observing and understanding your child more deeply, you start to respond to their needs with kindness and compassion. Instead of blaming them for not doing things they literally can't do yet, you help them build the skills they need to do it. Instead of shaming them for behaviors beyond their control, you comfort and console them, helping them feel loved. You interrupt the blame/shame game, and respond with safety and acceptance.

Imagine, for a moment, how powerful it can be to offer those same qualities to yourself.

I've experienced this myself. When I put these parenting practices in place, my sense of self-compassion increased over time. The more I practiced using kindness and respect with my kids—even when their behaviors drove me nuts—the more I noticed my internal voice was shifting. When I once would have said to myself, "What the heck is wrong with you?" I now say to myself, "Oh, honey. What's going on today?"

Remember repair? The ability to repair with our kids is a powerful tool to help them learn how to build better relationships throughout their lives. But it's also a powerful tool to heal ourselves. When we begin to put these practices into place on a regular basis, we start to forgive ourselves and our own worst behavior. It doesn't mean we accept it or ignore it, any more than we accept or ignore those behaviors in our kids. It means we ask ourselves what's under our own behavior, address our own unmet needs, and respond with love and kindness to ourselves.

So, when you're struggling, ask yourself the five questions:

1. What cues can I observe within myself?
2. What's happening with me? What about myself or my past might be at play?
3. Which of my needs aren't being met?
4. What's happening before, during, and after my behavior?
5. What can I change to help myself?

Over time, you'll find yourself building new habits that are infused with compassion and kindness toward your kids, yourself, and others in your life. You'll see that we all grow and change, and we all need understanding and acceptance. And eventually, you'll grow comfortable putting on that S.C.U.B.A. suit and taking a deeper dive, to see what's under the surface.

Putting it Into Practice: The S.C.U.B.A. Approach

Now that you know all the steps and the whys behind them, let's look at a few examples of how you could use the S.C.U.B.A. approach to dive deeper into a specific child's behavior.

Meet 2-year-old Mario.

Mario is a delightful child with two loving parents. His mom is getting frustrated, though, by a recent behavior he's picked up. In the mornings, he is slapping her in the face repeatedly—hard. She's understandably upset by it and isn't sure what to do. How can the S.C.U.B.A. approach help her?

See

Physiological cues: When she takes a closer look and really observes him in the moment, he seems happy and playful. He's smiling and laughing as he hits her each time.

Environmental cues: The slaps always happen in the bedroom. When she takes a moment to think through all the different senses, Mom realizes that the diaper pail deodorizer is quite strong in the room.

Time-related cues: The slaps seem to come almost always in the morning, before breakfast.

Child

Love: Mom is understandably upset that she's getting hit, and she's feeling hurt and disrespected. She takes a deep breath and reminds herself how much she loves Mario. She decides to focus on his smile and how delightful it is.

Development: Mario is 2 years old, and Mom knows his brain is still very underdeveloped. As much as it might feel like he's trying to hurt or manipulate her on purpose, she realizes he simply doesn't have the structures in place to do that. She also realizes that he can't yet take another person's perspective and his ability to empathize is still developing.

This kid: She has noticed that Mario tends to do a lot of things that give him proprioceptive input—he crashes into things, has difficulty giving gentle hugs, and squeezes every ounce of toothpaste out whenever he gets near a tube.

Under

Mom takes a breath and dives beneath the behavior to see what else might be going on. She finds some empathy herself as she realizes that he isn't trying to hurt her on purpose; he's trying to play.

Beneath his behavior:

She thinks about his sensory experiences in the moment and remembers the smell of the diaper pail. She wonders if that might be a stressor for him that he doesn't have words for. She also wonders if Mario slaps her so hard in order to get more proprioceptive input, which she knows tends to calm him down.

Beneath her behavior:

Mom takes a moment to think about why she's so upset, even while understanding that he's still a toddler. She remembers a bully in grade school who used to slap her as a way to humiliate her on the playground. She gives herself compassion as she remembers how hard that was and reminds herself that this is a different situation.

Behavior

Before:

Mario is consistently trying to climb out of his crib after waking. He goes between jumping in his crib to trying to climb over the rail.

During:

During Mario's behavior, he's smiling, he slaps his mom, then he laughs.

After:

She immediately says, "NO!" in a loud, stern voice, after which he usually slaps her again.

Adapt

Mom thinks about how she's answered the first four of the five questions:

1. What do I *see*? What cues can I observe?

    He doesn't seem upset. This always happens in the bedroom, where there's a strong smell. This always happens in the morning right after he wakes up and before breakfast.

2. What's happening with my *child*? Both developmentally and individually?
   She knows he's still too young to understand other perspectives or to have a deep sense of empathy. She also knows he seems to seek out proprioceptive input often.

3. What do I think is *under* this behavior? Which needs aren't being met?

   She wonders if the strong scent might be an unnamed stressor and if he's perhaps looking for more proprioceptive input to help calm himself.

4. What, exactly, is the *behavior*? What's happening before, during, and after?

   Before the slapping, he's often jumping or trying to climb out of his crib. He's slapping her hard in the moment, and after he repeats the behavior even when she has said, "NO!"

Now she's ready for question number five: What can I *adapt* or change? How can I help? She comes up with a plan of what to do.

Change the environment:

She decides to change how she stores dirty diapers and to use a different deodorizer.

Manage sensory input:

She will hold his hands and let him jump even more before lifting him out of the crib. She'll also wrap him tightly in a blanket and give him big squeezes and kisses when she does lift him out.

Shift tone:

She'll wake up ten minutes earlier so she can have a calming cup of tea in a quiet kitchen. She knows this will make her less likely to use a big, scary voice with him.

Adjust expectations:

She won't expect him to understand *why* slapping her isn't funny—at least not yet.

Reinforce boundaries:

She will be very clear when he does start to slap her that hitting is not okay. If he tries to slap, she'll grab and hold his hands while saying, "No hitting Mommy's face." She'll then redirect him to a behavior that's appropriate. "Here, we can play Patty Cake! Can you hit my hands?"

Mom tries all of these ideas for a couple of weeks. She realizes after the first week, he's stopped slapping her in the morning.

Meet 5-year-old Chelsea.

Chelsea started Kindergarten last week at a new dual-immersion language school. She enjoyed preschool, had lots of friends, and participated regularly. Now she won't easily separate from Dad when he drops her off. She clings and cries and has meltdowns like he hasn't seen in years. Dad's frustrated. She was perfectly fine being dropped off at preschool—what's going on now?

See

Physiological cues:

Chelsea's face is red when Dad tries to leave. Her breathing gets faster, and her eyes are wide with fright. When the teacher tries to pry her off of Dad, Chelsea collapses to the floor, staring blankly, and doesn't respond to the teacher.

Environmental cues:

The class is chaotic and loud as all the parents are dropping kids off at the same time. All the instructions from the teacher are in Spanish, and Chelsea is not familiar with that language yet.

Time-related cues:

This is always in the morning, after breakfast and driving to school.

Child

Love:

Dad reminds himself how much he loves Chelsea. He thinks about how much she likes to dance with him on the weekends.

Development:

Chelsea is 5, and while she did do well being dropped off at her previous preschool, this is a new environment for her. It's not unusual for children this age to cling to their parents when they're in a new place with new people and expectations are still unclear. She's also trying to take in information that's in an entirely different language. While she's young and will become fluent quickly, it will still take time for her brain to begin processing in a second language.

This kid:

Chelsea is usually confident in herself and made friends easily in preschool. For her to collapse, be quiet, and not respond is extremely unusual for her.

Under

Beneath her behavior:

Dad takes a breath and dives beneath the behavior to see what else might be going on. He realizes that she is truly distressed when he leaves her at school and that her response is overwhelming for her. He also thinks about the chaotic environment and wonders if that might be contributing to the problem.

Beneath his behavior:

Dad thinks about how frustrated he's getting with Chelsea. He recalls being punished when he was a "cry baby," as his parents called it. That definitely did not make him feel better, and he finds compassion for himself as he processes those memories. He now finds a little extra empathy for Chelsea. He sees that she needs his help and resolves to work with her instead of against her.

Behavior

Before:

They drive to school, park, and walk inside. Chelsea starts chewing on her shirt as soon as they get to the classroom.

During:

Chelsea cries and screams loudly, almost as if she's trying to be heard above the noise. She clings to Dad's leg tightly. When the teacher comes to pull her so Dad can leave, she collapses to the floor with a blank look on her face.

After:

The teacher reports that she remains quiet most of the day, refuses to participate in class, and chews on her shirt constantly.

Adapt

Dad thinks about how he's answered the first four of the five questions:

1. What do I *see*? What cues can I observe?

    Chelsea is distraught and overwhelmed in an unfamiliar and chaotic environment. She's also dealing with trying to learn a new language on top of that. That's a challenging way to start anyone's morning!
2. What's happening with my *child*? Both developmentally and individually?

    It's not unusual for Kindergarteners to have trouble separating from their parents at the beginning of the year, especially if they're trying to learn a new language. For Chelsea to shut down like this isn't like her, and it will only make it harder for her to learn all the things she needs to feel successful.

3. What do I think is *under* this behavior? What needs aren't being met?

    Chelsea clearly needs Dad's help. He doesn't want her to feel like he did when he struggled as a kid.

4. What exactly is the *behavior*? What's happening before, during, and after?

    Even on the way into class she's chewing her shirt, which tells Dad that she's feeling anxious. When Dad has to leave, Chelsea is clinging to his leg and then shutting down when the teacher pulls her away. She's withdrawn the rest of the day and chews on her shirt consistently.

Now he's ready for question number five: What can I *adapt* or change? How can I help? He comes up with a plan of what to do.

Change the environment:

While Dad can't change the environment, he can change the timing. He talks to the teacher, and they decide he'll arrive with Chelsea a bit earlier so she has more time with the teacher in a quieter classroom.

Manage sensory input:

Since Chelsea is chewing when she's feeling anxious, which gives proprioceptive input, Dad gets her a special necklace she can chew on.

Shift tone:

Dad will remember that she needs help at drop-off and take a softer tone. He'll also work with the teacher to leave before things get busy so Chelsea has time to bond with the teacher on her own.

Adjust expectations:

Dad won't expect her to have the same behaviors now that she did in preschool. He'll expect that this may take a while, and that she'll need some extra support.

Reinforce boundaries:

Dad will consistently take Chelsea to school a little earlier every morning until she feels more comfortable. He and the teacher agree she won't be pried off of his leg anymore, and they'll find something she enjoys, like Playdough, when it's time for him to leave. Chelsea will learn that school is not a choice and that Dad does need to leave each day, but also that school is a safe place and her needs will be met.

Dad tries all of these ideas for a couple of weeks. In the second week, Chelsea starts to go to the Playdough table without tears when it's time for him to go. The teacher reports that, while Chelsea isn't chatty, she is starting to participate. He decides to continue this plan until the teacher reports she's acting more like herself and socializing with other kids.

Meet 10-year-old Luther.

Luther had some recent health challenges and now needs to get his blood drawn once a week. Every time he's in the doctor's office he melts down, crying and refusing to sit still. Mom is scared he's going to get hurt, but she's more scared of what will happen if they don't get the bloodwork done. She hates to force him, but the last two times she had to hold him down alongside a nurse. What's the right thing to do?

See

Physiological cues:

Luther's heart is racing, his face is red, and his cheeks are wet with tears when he's in the room. When he's being held down, he's screaming incoherently and thrashing.

Environmental cues:

The room is large with lots of chairs and other people having their blood drawn. Everyone stops and stares at him when he starts to freak out.

Time-related cues:

The blood work must be done before he eats. Sometimes they can't get an appointment until an hour or two after he usually has breakfast.

Child

Love:

Mom takes a breath and remembers the sweet way Luther helps at home and how kind he is with his younger sister.

Development:

Luther is tall for his age, but he's still only 10 years old. While he has the ability to control his emotions in many circumstances, it's not unusual for him to lose it in this situation. The thought of the needle is terrifying, which ignites his stress response. Mom remembers that when the stress response is activated, access to the part of his brain that regulates emotions is very limited, even in adults.

This kid:

Luther has never liked getting shots, but this whole incident started with a trip to the emergency room. He and his mom were both terrified at the time, and that was when they did his first blood draw.

Under

Beneath his behavior:

When mom thinks more about things, she realizes that Luther may already be feeling out of control and unsafe—and holding him down only increases those feelings.

Beneath her behavior:

Mom realizes that she is feeling scared, as well. The hospital visit was traumatizing for both of them, and she is probably communicating some of her fear to him every time they go in for a blood draw.

Behavior

Before:

Luther starts complaining even before they leave the house, trying to delay going out the door.

During:

Luther cries and tries to get out of the chair. When he's being held down, he escalates and begins screaming and writhing while they take his blood.

After:

Luther is silent and withdrawn as they leave, oftentimes not wanting to eat breakfast even though he must be hungry.

Adapt

Mom thinks about how she's answered the first four of the five questions:

1. What do I *see*? What cues can I observe?

    Luther is clearly terrified during these times, feeling out of control and unsafe.

2. What's happening with my *child*? Both developmentally and individually?

    Even though he's able to regulate his emotions most of the time, his stress response shuts down the part of his brain that enables him to do that. He's also never been a fan of shots, but the trip to the hospital was really frightening.

3. What do I think is *under* this behavior? What needs aren't being met?

> Luther is terrified, and when he's being held down that feeling amplifies. He needs to feel safe and comforted so that he can use the coping skills he's learned.

4. What exactly is the *behavior*? What's happening before, during, and after?

> Luther tries to delay leaving for the clinic. When he's there, he's crying and trying to escape, which turns to screaming and frantically writhing while he's being restrained.

Now she's ready for question number five: What can I *adapt* or change? How can I help? She comes up with a plan.

Change the environment:

Mom wonders if all the people watching makes it worse. She decides to talk with the doctor about finding a more private space for blood draws.

Mom also realizes that holding Luther down is making things worse, not better. She will also speak with the doctor and staff about finding ways to let Luther feel like he has more control.

Manage sensory input:

Mom wonders if Luther is feeling overwhelmed in the moment. She knows that he finds music soothing, so she decides to let him listen to his headphones in the car as well as during the blood draw, if he wants. She'll also have some funny videos ready for him to watch to distract him from his internal senses—especially of the pain of the needle going in.

In addition, she'll start to carry something he can eat immediately afterward in case hunger is part of the problem. She'll make it something special, like his favorite granola bar.

Shift tone:

Mom will work on her own feelings of fear so she's not bringing them into the situation. She reminds herself that he's out of the hospital, and that this monitoring is what will keep him healthy. She decides to repeat to herself the phrase, "He's okay now," to help keep her in the moment and stop reliving the past hospital event.

Adjust expectations:

Mom will not expect him to be able to control his emotions when he's so scared. She'll expect the clinic staff to work with both of them to find ways to lessen his fears and increase his feelings of control.

Reinforce boundaries:

While Mom will work with the medical team to help Luther feel safer, she will also make sure that he continues to get regular blood draws. She'll speak to him throughout the week to give him the chance to talk about his worries or fears and let him know that she will help him through this. She'll also reinforce that in order to keep him safe and healthy right now, this is what the doctor needs them to do.

Mom tries all of this. She and the medical team decide to draw his blood in a private room away from others. They also agree to not hold him down. Instead, they use distraction and let him choose to listen to his music or watch a funny video on her phone during the blood draw. If he starts to panic, everything stops while the adults help him use some deep breathing techniques to calm down. It takes a few more weeks, but after about a month he has stopped screaming and crying during the blood draws. He still dislikes them, but he is able to tolerate them.

Conclusion

Every parent knows just how hard of a gig this is. An ever-changing exercise in patience, being a parent is both the most rewarding and frustrating job in the world. Remember that you're not alone. Every parent goes through rough patches, and there's simply no one perfect way to do this.

But you can empower yourself with this concept:

See your
Child
Under their
Behavior and
Adapt

You are moving forward in a way that will build the tools you need to recognize and meet your child's needs. You are building confidence in your parenting and reinforcing a forcefield that repels all the unasked for advice that can rain down on you in the worst moments. You are building a relationship with your child that will be the foundation for a secure attachment, setting them up for success throughout the rest of their life.

You're also building the muscles of compassion, for your child, for yourself—for the world, really. Once you begin to practice this approach regularly, it will become second nature for you to take a step back and peek at what's going on under the surface when conflict arises with family, friends and colleagues. You'll step out of that blame-shame game and start to see others as they truly are: imperfect, vulnerable human beings who struggle.

I've included templates you can use to gather specifics about challenging behaviors and fill your cup, examples of ways to get different kinds of sensory input, and a list of other resources you may find helpful (much of which I used to write this book). As you move forward, remember that you will make mistakes. Celebrate them. Learn from them. Share that process with your child so they learn the art of repair. Over time, you'll both learn how to be more authentic, vulnerable, compassionate, and resilient.

Remember that in this S.C.U.B.A. dive, you can breathe deeply without an apparatus and enjoy the journey without fear of failure. What you find in the depths of yourself, your child, and your relationship will be priceless.

Your Turn!

Take a moment to think about a recent behavior that's been bothering you. Write it down here. Don't worry about being too detailed—just write a quick summary.

_____
_____
_____
_____

Now go through the S.C.U.B.A. approach:

See

Physiological cues:

_____
_____

Environmental cues:

_____
_____

Time-related cues:

_____
_____

Child

Love:

_____
_____

Development:

_____
_____

This kid:

_____
_____

Under

Their behavior:

_____
_____

Your behavior:

_____
_____

Behavior

Before:

_____
_____

During:

_____
_____

After:

_____
_____

Adapt

Think about how you've answered the first four of the five questions:

1. What do I *See*? What cues can I observe?

   _____
   _____

2. What's happening with my *Child*? Both developmentally and individually?

   _____
   _____

3. What do I think is *Under* this behavior? What needs aren't being met?

_____
_____

4. What, exactly, is the *Behavior*? What's happening before, during, and after?

_____
_____

Now you're ready for question number five: What can I *Adapt* or change? How can I help? Come up with a plan of what to do.

Change the environment:

_____
_____

Manage sensory input:

_____
_____

Shift tone:

_____
_____

Adjust expectations:

_____
_____

Reinforce boundaries:

_____
_____

Try this plan for at least two weeks and observe what changes.

My Cup-Fillers

What fills your cup?

Here are some ideas to get you started—write down a few that work for you.

Hot tea/coffee	Reading
Walking	Dancing
Jogging	Music
Meditation/Prayer	Napping

_____
_____

What support do you need to make this work?

Again, here are a few ideas to get you thinking.

Childcare	Help with dishes
Earlier wake-up time	Transportation
Space to move	Walking buddy

_____
_____

PLAN it!

As you look at this list, which can you do on a regular basis? Try to find one you can do every day, and one you can do every week. Be specific! Then put it in your calendar.

Every day I will _____ at _____ a.m./p.m.

Every week I will _____ at _____ a.m./p.m. on _____ day.

Sensory Input Ideas

As you consider how you'll adapt things to meet your child's needs, here are some ideas regarding sensory input. Sometimes kids may need more input, and sometimes they may need less input. Remember it's an experiment! SEE how things go, and make changes as needed. I've put some space for notes to help get you into the practice of observing your child before, during, and after any sensory activity.

Sight

More input:
    brightly colored posters, toys on display, mazes, hidden picture puzzles
Less input:
    bare walls, clear shelves and tables, consistent neutral colors

Notes on how they were *before*:
_____
_____

Notes on how they were *during*:
_____
_____

Notes on how they were *after*:
_____
_____

Sound

More input:
> music, instruments, nature sounds, concert, storytime

Less input:
> ear protectors, white noise, "quiet corner," gentle background music

Notes on how they were *before*:
_____
_____

Notes on how they were *during*:
_____
_____

Notes on how they were *after*:
_____
_____

Smell

More input:
    scented playdough, baking, aromatherapy diffuser, cut up fruit salad
Less input:
    scent-free cleaning and laundry products, ventilation, outdoor time

Notes on how they were *before*:
_____
_____

Notes on how they were *during*:
_____
_____

Notes on how they were *after*:
_____
_____

Touch

More input:
    sensory bin, finger painting, cooking, nature walk
Less input:
    avoid itchy labels or fabrics, limit tags and seams on clothing

Notes on how they were *before*:
_____
_____

Notes on how they were *during*:
_____
_____

Notes on how they were *after*:
_____
_____

Taste

More input:
    flavor comparisons using tea, popsicles, or herbs
Less input:
    bland snacks, minimal seasonings, drinking water

Notes on how they were *before*:
_____
_____

Notes on how they were *during*:
_____
_____

Notes on how they were *after*:
_____
_____

Vestibular (balance)

More input:
> swinging, rocking chairs, balance board, bicycle riding

Less input:
> stable seats with support, slow movement like yoga

Notes on how they were *before*:
_____
_____

Notes on how they were *during*:
_____
_____

Notes on how they were *after*:
_____
_____

Proprioception (body awareness)

More input:
      pushing/pulling heavy things, weighted blankets, playing with clay, gum

Less input:
      lightweight clothing and blankets, calm transitions, gentle water play

Notes on how they were *before*:
_____
_____

Notes on how they were *during*:
_____
_____

Notes on how they were *after*:
_____
_____

Interoception (internal sense)

More input:
>	mindful breathing, paying attention to heartbeat, mindful eating

Less input:
>	distraction, nature or external observations, soothing music to focus on

Notes on how they were *before*:
_____
_____

Notes on how they were *during*:
_____
_____

Notes on how they were *after*:
_____
_____

Resources

Becoming the Parent You Want to Be: A Sourcebook of Strategies for the First Five Years, by Laura Davis and Janis Keyser.

Behave: The Biology of Humans at Our Best and Worst, by Robert Sapolsky.

Brain-Body Parenting: How to Stop Managing Behavior and Start Raising Joyful, Resilient Kids, by Mona Delahooke, Ph.D.

Good Inside: A Guide to Becoming the Parent You Want to Be, by Dr. Becky Kennedy.

How to Talk So Kids Will Listen & Listen So Kids Will Talk, by Adele Faber and Elaine Mazlish.

Mindset: The New Psychology of Success, by Carol S. Dweck, Ph.D.

No Drama Discipline: The Whole-Brain Way to Calm the Chaos and Nurture Your Child's Developing Brain, by Dan Siegel, M.D. and Tina Payne Bryson, Ph.D.

The Out-Of-Sync Child: Recognizing and Coping with Sensory Processing Differences, by Carol Stock Kranowitz, MA.

Parenting from the Inside Out, by Dan Siegel, M.D., and Mary Hartzell, M.Ed.

The Reflective Parent: How to Do Less and Relate More with Your Kids, by Regina Pally, M.D.

Smart but Scattered: The Revolutionary "Executive Skills" to Helping Kids Reach Their Potential, by Peg Dawson, Ed.D. and Richard Guare, Ph.D.

The Whole-Brain Child: 12 Revolutionary Strategies to Nurture Your Child's Developing Mind, by Dan Siegel, M.D. and Tina Payne Bryson, Ph.D.

Coming Soon from Kristene Geering:

A practical guide to build self-regulation skills with a sensory-based approach.

www.ingramcontent.com/pod-product-compliance
Lightning Source LLC
Chambersburg PA
CBHW071239090426
42736CB00014B/3139